50 FANTASTIC SCIENCE JOBS

Written by Tom Jackson

WAYLAND

CONTENTS

JOBS IN BIOLOGY

Botanist 6-7
Zoologist 8-9
Primatologist 10-11
Ecologist 12-13
Molecular Biologist 14-15
Mycologist 16-17
Entomologist 18-19
Microbiologist 20-21
Ichthyologist 22-23
Virologist 24-25
Geneticist 26-27
Herpetologist 28-29
Ornithologist 30-31

JOBS IN PHYSICS

Cosmologist 34-35
Astrophysicist 36-37
Quantum Physicist 38-39
Particle Physicist 40-41
Astronomer 42-43
Metrologist 44-45
Meteorologist 46-47
Acoustician 48-49
Optical Scientist 50-51
Materials Scientist 52-53
Climate Scientist 54-55
Condensed Matter Physicist ......
.... 56-57

JOBS IN CHEMISTRY

Biochemist 60-61	*Physcial Chemist* 74-75
Chemical Engineer 62-63	*Nanotechnologist* 76-77
Analytical Chemist 64-65	*Computational Chemist* ... 78-79
Toxicologist 66-67	*Nuclear Chemist* 80-81
Pharmacologist 68-69	*Lab Technician* 82-83
Organic Chemist 70-71	
Foresnsic Scientist 72-73	

JOBS IN TECHNOLOGY AND ENGINEERING

Mechanical Engineer 86-87	*Epidemiologist* 100-101
Electrical Engineer 88-89	*Network Engineer* 102-103
Aerospace Engineer 90-91	*Web Developer* 104-105
Construction Engineer 92-93	*Sports Technologist* 106-107
Microchip Engineer 94-95	*Software Developer* ... 108-109
Cryptographer 96-97	*Roboticist* 110-111
Genetic Engineer 98-99	*INDEX* 112

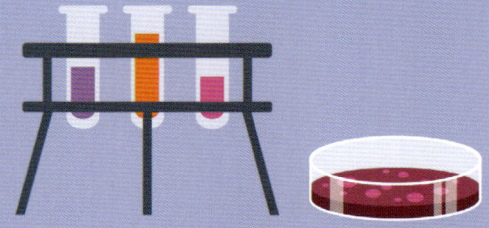

JOBS IN ...
BIOLOGY

Do you want to work with the most unusual animals and plants in the Universe? If so, become an expert in biology, the science of living things.

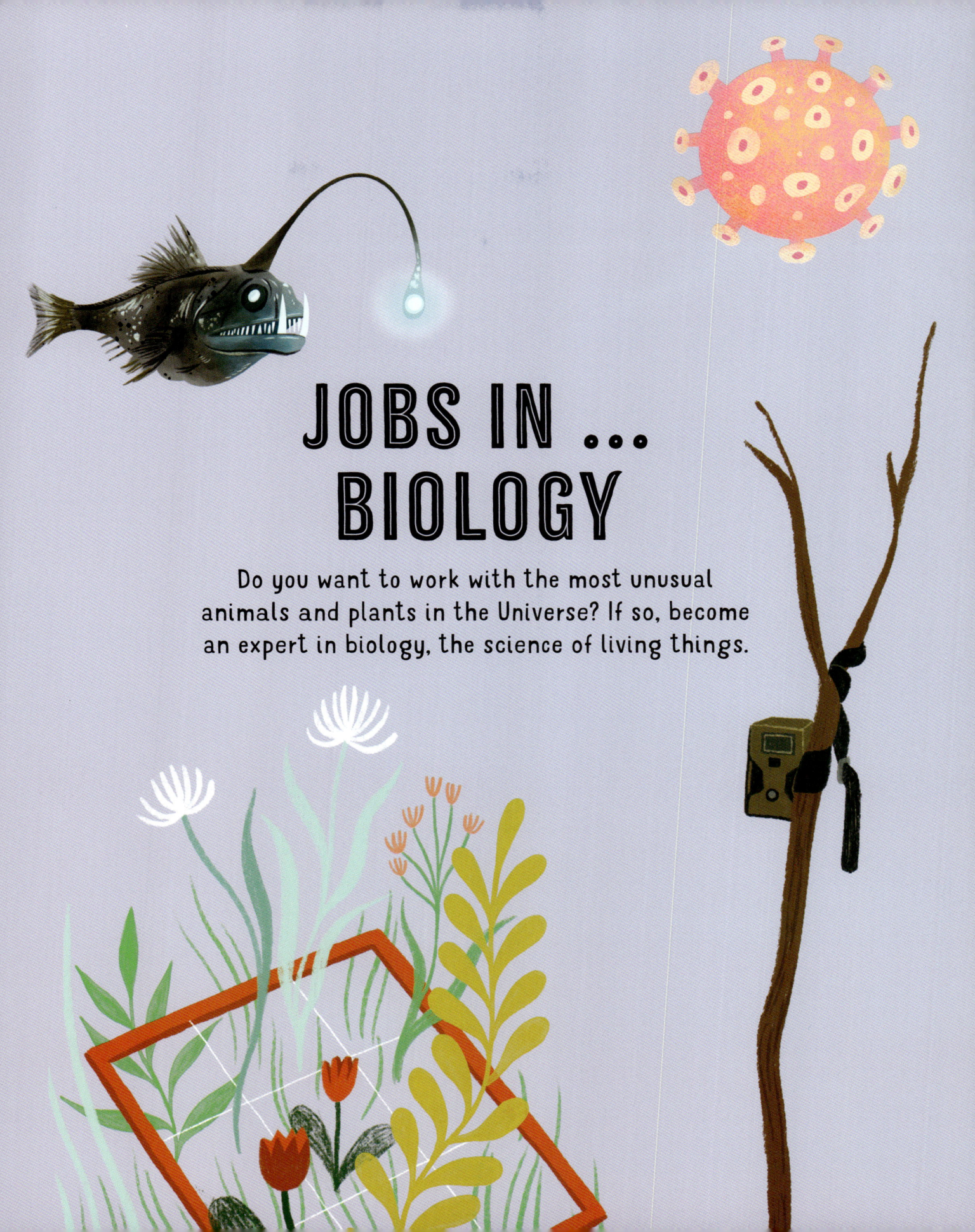

BOTANIST

What does a Botanist do?

A botanist studies plants, searching the world to find new kinds of tree or flower and figure out how they grow in different habitats.

A botanist is an expert in the way plants live. They are able to tell one plant from another from the shape of their leaves, flowers and fruits. Plants come in all sizes and shapes from immense forest trees to tiny herbs. They survive in many different ways, from a cactus in a desert to a mangrove tree growing out of the sea. It is a botanist's job to figure out how they do it.

They study plant anatomy which means they look closely at every part of the plant inside and out, often using a microscope to see the different kinds of cell. The scientists also grow plants collected from different places in botanical gardens. There they can measure how fast they sprout and do experiments to find out more about each plant's life cycle.

KEY SKILLS:

Attention to detail – Botanists need to spot the small differences between one species of plant and another.

Drawing skills – Often a botanist will make sketches of new plants they find: photography skills are also useful.

Being patient – Some botany experiments take years to complete: that's how long it takes the plants to grow!

A love of nature – Botanists spend a long time in wild places, collecting samples and making surveys.

ZOOLOGIST

What does a Zoologist do?

A zoologist studies all animals, looking to see how they live differently from other kinds of life and investigating how they have evolved to survive all over the world.

A zoologist might work at a zoo, which is short for 'zoological garden', and is a place full of animals for the public to see. However, zoologists do a lot more than that because animal biology is a huge subject with millions of different kinds of animals to study.

Zoologists are especially interested in evolution, which is the way living things change very gradually over millions of years to adapt to live in different ways. Zoologists compare the animals that are living today to figure out how they are related. Zoologists also work on understanding animal behaviour. For example, they set up remote-controlled cameras in the wild to capture the sights and sounds of animals that are normally too shy to come near to people.

KEY SKILLS:

A love of animals – Zoologists spend a lot of time out in the wild observing animals and collecting samples.

Imaginative – Zoologists think of new ways to explain what they see animals doing and then come up with ways to test these ideas.

Mathematical skills – Zoologists use mathematics to make sense of the data they collect on animal behaviour.

Liking complex ideas – Zoology involves understanding complicated things, such as how species evolve and how different bodies work.

PRIMATOLOGIST

What does a Primatologist do?

A primatologist studies apes and monkeys, our closest animal relatives, trying to understand how they behave.

Primates are a group of animals that includes monkeys, lemurs and apes – and human beings. A primatologist is an expert in these animals, which often live in complicated social groups. By learning about how primates live, primatologists help us understand about how our species might have evolved over millions of years.

Primatologists spend a lot of time watching monkeys and apes and record what they do. They are especially interested in chimpanzees and gorillas, which are our two closest relatives. The scientists might travel to remote jungles and watch animals in the wild. They also work in zoos and nature reserves, where the animals are protected but still live in natural ways.

* *

KEY SKILLS:

Organisational skills – Primatologists have to write down everything that the animals do, and in a way that other scientists can understand.

Enjoy the outdoors – These scientists spend a long time in nature. Some of them live in the jungle for years.

Mathematical skills – Primatologists use a kind of mathematics called statistics to understand animal behaviour.

A good imagination – Primatologists must come up with clever ways to test their ideas about the ways monkeys and apes behave.

ECOLOGIST

What does an Ecologist do?

An ecologist studies ecosystems, which are complicated communities of wild plants and animals that occupy different habitats.

An ecologist is interested in how living things survive in their home environment, or habitat. To survive, each species of animal, plant, fungus and even microbe has to find food and a place to live - and avoid becoming the food of another member of the ecosystem! Ecologists visit different habitats and gather as much information as they can. They survey what is living there by collecting samples and counting how many different kinds of life they see.

They also gather weather and climate data and see how the ecosystems change throughout the day and the year. Sadly, many natural habitats are damaged by human activity and pollution. A big part of an ecologist's job is figuring out how the ecosystem is changing because of this, and how we can help protect nature.

KEY SKILLS:

Physical resilience – Ecologists work hard in extreme environments. They may spend months at a time in freezing Antarctica or work in steamy jungles, hot deserts, or soggy swamps.

Diverse knowlege – Ecologists are interested in all kinds of life and they also need to know about geography, chemistry and physics to understand each ecosystem.

Mathematical skills – Ecosystems are complicated systems, and ecologists use mathematics to make predictions about how they change.

Conservation – Ecology is an important science in protecting the natural world from the damage humans are doing.

MOLECULAR BIOLOGIST

What does a Molecular Biologist do?

A molecular biologist studies the many chemical molecules that are made inside cells and spread around the body to keep organisms alive.

Life can be seen as a complicated set of chemical reactions that are happening inside the body. These chemical reactions turn the molecules in our food into other substances that are needed to keep our bodies alive and healthy. This chemical activity is called metabolism.

A molecular biologist is an expert in these many reactions – there are billions of them happening inside you every second! Molecular biologists work in laboratories where they use specialist machines to perform chemical tests. One of the most important molecules in the body is DNA, which is the chemical that holds our genes. Each gene is an instruction on how to make another molecule called a protein. The protein is then used as a metabolic machine for making useful things. Molecular biologists work to figure out how all these molecules are created. This means they can help people who are sick due to problems with their metabolism.

KEY SKILLS:

Chemistry skills — Molecular biologists are experts in chemistry as well as biology.

Perserverance — Molecular biologists must carry out a lot of different tests and experiments to make discoveries.

Analytical skills — Molecular biologists try to figure out what is happening from the changes in the chemicals they find.

Interest in many fields — Molecular biology has links to all other areas of biology, and molecular biologists are interested in them all!

MYCOLOGIST

What does a Mycologist do?

A mycologist is a scientist that studies fungi, such as toadstools and mushrooms, which are a completely separate type of life from plants and animals.

Finding fungi can be harder than finding plants and animals, they are often hidden away or not immediately visisble. Fungi live everywhere from the soil to the sea. Their seedlike spores are floating in the air and some are even living on you as well! Fungi are an important part of ecosystems because they are the organisms that make dead plants and animals rot away back into soil. Mycologists are also involved in creating new medicines. Some of the most important medicines, such as antibiotics, came from studying fungi.

Experts in fungi can also work for food and drink companies. Fungi called yeast is used to make bread, beer and meat-free foods. One day, mycologists might also be making clean low-carbon fuels from fungi.

KEY SKILLS:

Micropscope skills — Mycologists spend a lot of time looking at microscopic details of fungal spores and cells.

Sharing ideas — Mycologists, like all scientists, share what they have discovered. It helps others come up with new ideas to investigate.

Careful worker — Mycologists carry out many complicated experiments in the lab and need to get each one right.

Innovative thinking — Mycology is a growing science, and becoming increasingly useful in the development of medicines.

ENTOMOLOGIST

What does an Entomologist do?

An entomologist is an expert on insects, which are the most common type of animals on the planet!

Nine out of ten animal species are insects. They include honeybees, butterflies, and beetles – if it has six legs, then it's probably an insect. There are 1.4 billion insects for every person on Earth and, when added up, all those insects weigh 70 times as much as all of us. That means entomologists are probably studying the most important type of animal on Earth!

Entomologists are still discovering new insect species; there are more than a million of them. They capture insects from all around the world and take a close look at them, often using a microscope, to see if they are a brand new species. Insects have complicated life cycles, so an entomologist will study a new species to see how they grow from an egg into an adult, what food they eat, and how they fit into the ecosystem.

KEY SKILLS:

Interest in agriculture – Entomologists help to devise ways to protect crops and farm animals from attack by pest insects.

Detective skills – Entomologists can help the police to understand what insects they find at crime scenes, and what they might mean.

Attention to detail – There are so many types of insect, entomologists need to examine all the details to tell one species from another.

Insect handling – Entomologists handle all kinds of creepy-crawlies, grubs and maggots.

MICROBIOLOGIST

What does a Microbiologist do?

A microbiologist is interested in life forms that are too small to see without a microscope, which includes bacteria, tiny plantlike algae, and miniature animals.

Microbiologists are experts at using different types of microscopes to get a close look at tiny organisms. These include minute worms that live in soil, and shrimplike crustaceans that live in the ocean, plus single-celled organisms such as amoebas and bacteria. Most microscopes use beams of light to magnify images, and microbiologists will add coloured dyes to show up different features in their samples.

Light microscopes allow microbiologists to observe microorganisms that are still alive. To see closer still, microbiologists use electron microscopes, which use beams of electrons to see right inside the cells that make up all living bodies. Microbiologists may work with drug companies to make medicines for diseases caused by microorganisms, and they are also working in new biotechnologies where bacteria are used to make useful chemicals.

KEY SKILLS:

Careful worker – Microbiologists work with organisms that are too small to see and therefore must be good at keeping clear records of samples.

Problem solver – Often microbiologists work with organisms that cause disease or other serious problems.

Teaching others – Microbiologists help non-scientists understand how microorganisms can be helpful as well as harmful.

Interested in new ideas – Microbiologists are searching for ways that microorganisms can be used in new technologies.

ICHTHYOLOGIST

What does an Ichthyologist do?

An ichthyologist studies fish, searching for new species, investigating where they live in oceans or rivers, and checking if they are endangered.

There are about 30,000 species of fish and that includes everything from the fish that we eat, such as tuna and anchovies, to giant sharks and colourful reef fish. Ichthyologists are experts in the anatomy, or body structure of fish, and can tell how the animal swims and where it lives from the shape of its body and position of its fins. There are fish living wherever there is enough water and food, including the deepest seabeds and even underground rivers running through caves.

Ichthyologists collect examples of fish from all these places, hoping to find a new species. They travel the oceans on research ships, using nets to catch fish, and sometimes they even travel deep underwater themselves inside submersibles. Ichthyologists study the lifecycles of fish species, which is important for understanding how fish populations are affected by fishing fleets and climate change.

KEY SKILLS:

Understanding mathematics – Fish populations go up and down fast, and ichthyologists use complicated mathematics to keep track of them.

Attention to detail – Ichthyologists examine fish carefully and make exact measurements so they can tell one species from another.

Drawing skills – Ichthyologists will often make sketches of fish body parts and use cameras to capture photos and videos of fish.

Teaching others – Ichthyologists share what they know about fish and what that tells us about oceans and rivers to help people protect nature.

VIROLOGIST

What does a Virologist do?

A virologist is an expert in viruses, which are complex packets of chemicals that cause diseases like measles and covid.

A virologist looks at some of the smallest things in biology. Viruses are so small that it is hard to see them clearly even with an electron microscope. As well as using microscopes, virologists study viruses by looking at the unique set of chemicals inside them.

Viruses are not living things. Instead, they are made from DNA and other chemicals that are able to take over a cell by hacking into its control system. Virologists study how each virus does this and figure out ways to stop it happening with medicines and vaccines. Some virologists are medical doctors who are experts in treating human diseases, but others study viruses that attack other life forms, such as plants and bacteria.

KEY SKILLS:

Applying knowledge – A virologist can save millions of lives by using their knowledge to prevent diseases.

Micropscope skills – One of the first jobs of a virologist is to look at a new virus through a microscope to find out what type it is.

Interest in chemistry – Viruses are packets of complicated chemicals, and virologists will investigate each one of them.

Developing new ideas – Virology has many uses, from creating new medicines and chemicals to genetic engineering.

GENETICIST

What does a Geneticist do?

A geneticist studies how all the instructions for building a living body are stored as special codes called genes in a chemical called DNA.

A geneticist is an expert on how the information needed for a new body to grow is passed on from parents to their children. This is a process called inheritance, and the information is stored in chemical codes, called genes, which you get from your parents. Geneticists understand how the code is stored in a complicated chemical called DNA, or deoxyribonucleic acid.

They work in a laboratory to decode DNA samples, and then try to work out what those samples mean. It is a very big job, with a lot still to learn. Humans alone have 20,000 genes. Geneticists help people with diseases caused by bad genes. They also study how a body grows and how evolution has changed genes over and over again to make many new species of living thing.

* *

KEY SKILLS:

Having big ideas – Geneticists are looking for new ways to understand how all life works. Their discoveries might change the world one day!

Helping others – A geneticist can help people with problematic genes to live a healthy and happy life.

Using imagination – Genetics involves chemicals working together and we can never see it actually happen. Geneticists are good at following the invisible process.

Mathematical skills – Geneticists collect information about inheritance from large numbers of people and use mathematics to make sense of the data.

HERPETOLOGIST

What does a Herpetologist do?

A herpetologist studies reptiles and amphibians, which includes everything from snakes and crocodiles to tadpoles and newts.

A herpetologist is interested in everything about reptiles and amphibians, including how their bodies work, how they behave and how they fit into ecosystems. Herpetologists work in the field, collecting and recording the frogs, lizards and snakes that they find in different habitats. New species are discovered all the time.

Herpetologists also carry out experiments in the lab. It is often easier to keep small reptiles and amphibians in captivity than other animals, and the scientists study their life cycle and behaviours, and the way these are affected by changes in the environment. Herpetologists have discovered that changes to the wild populations of amphibians and reptiles are important early signals that their ecosystem has a problem.

KEY SKILLS:

Care for animals – Herpetologists keep animals like frogs and lizards for breeding and use in experiments and they must treat them well.

Love of wild places – Herpetologists travel to wild areas to observe the reptiles and amphibians that live there.

Confidence with animals – Herpetologists may have to handle dangerous animals such as venomous snakes and fierce crocodiles.

Good record-keeping – Herpetologists must gather information in a clear way from experiments and surveys of wild habitats.

ORNITHOLOGIST

What does an Ornithologist do?

An ornithologist is a scientist that is a specialist in understanding birds, including how they fly, build nests and communicate.

Ornithologists spend a lot of time outside looking for birds. They know how to search for each species by listening for their songs or targeting a certain habitat. The scientists have powerful binoculars for seeing birds from far away.

Ornithologists do important work to keep bird populations safe from things like airports, wind turbines, and damaging farming practices. They also monitor migrations by catching wild birds and fitting them with harmless numbered rings. The rings allow the scientists to keep records of the birds as they fly from place to place each year. Larger birds are fitted with tiny radio trackers so ornithologists can see the route they take to their breeding grounds each year. This helps to ensure that the birds have enough wild habitat along the way to keep making the journey, year after year.

KEY SKILLS:

Patience – Ornithologists need to be patient to locate and observe birds.

Good with animals – Ornithologist may breed rare birds and then release them into the wild.

Communication – Ornithologists help explain how human activities are changing nature and what we can do about it.

Analytical skills – Ornithologists must analyse the data they collect to find out what it can tell us about the way birds live.

JOBS IN ... PHYSICS

Do you want to be an expert in how the world really works? Then you should think about becoming a physicist. They study the rules and laws that explain everything!

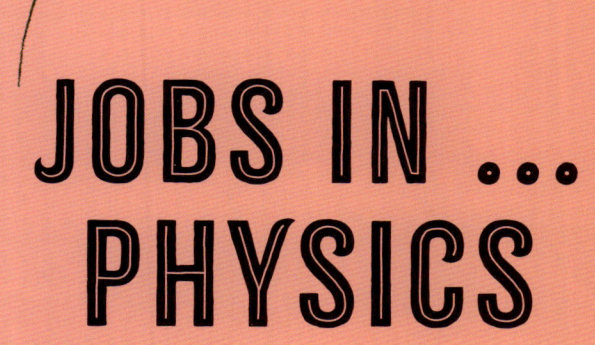
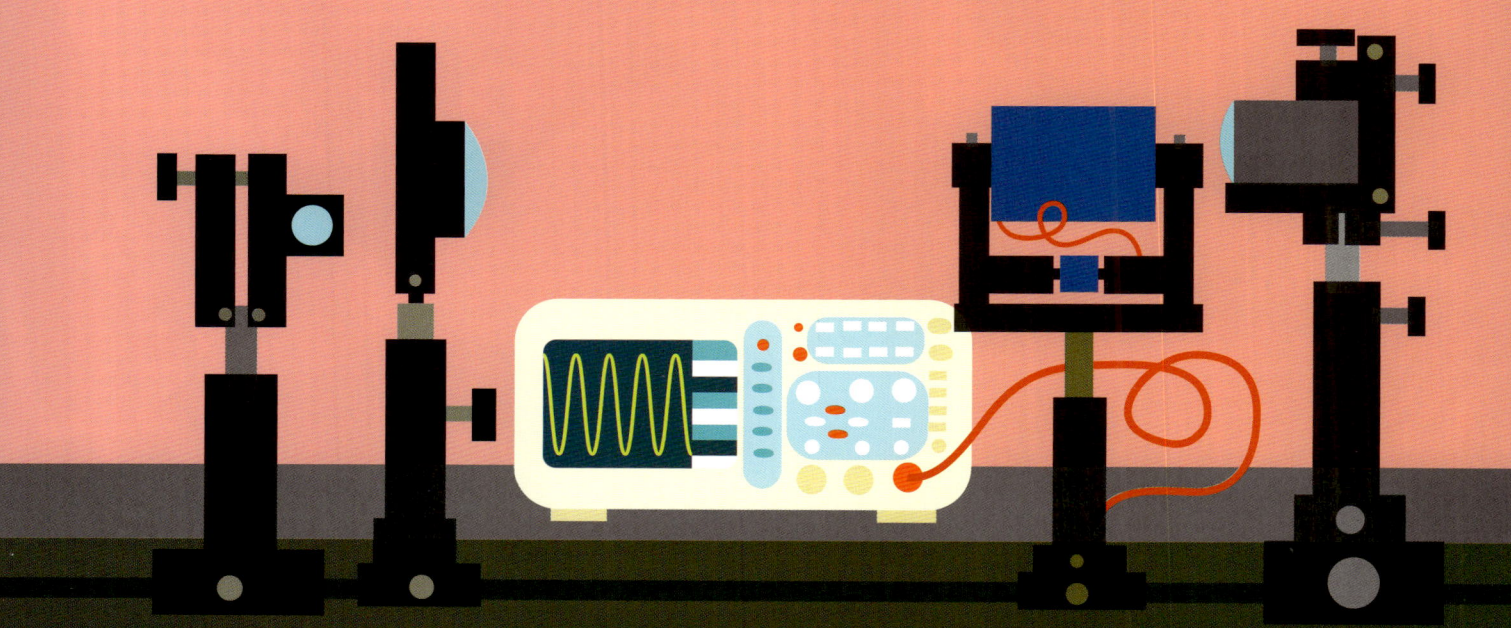

COSMOLOGIST

What does a Cosmologist do?

Cosmologists wants to find out how the Universe – and everything in it – came to be. They also investigate how the Universe is changing.

Cosmologists are trying to solve several big mysteries, inlcuding dark energy which is making the space expand very fast; dark matter, which is stuff that is very heavy but completely invisible; and the Big Bang, which is when the Universe started. To find answers, a cosmologist comes up with a theory, which is an idea that might explain a mystery about the Universe. They then need to test this idea and often that means creating very large and elaborate experiments. These experiments may be carried out on board space probes or buried deep underground. Some are even based at the South Pole!

Cosmologists also use supercomputers to create models of the Universe. These models help them understand why the Universe is the way it is – and perhaps how it will be very different one day in the far, far future.

* *

KEY SKILLS:

Being patient – Cosmology experiments can take many years to get started, and then they may not get results for many more years!

Working in a team – To come up with new theories, cosmologists must work with many different experts.

Mathematical skills – Mathematics is used a lot in cosmology to help understand energy, light and space.

Teaching – Cosmology is important but complicated, and so cosmologists have to spend a lot of time explaining it to other people.

ASTROPHYSICIST

What does an Astrophysicist do?

An astrophysicist studies stars and investigates how they form, what is happening inside the star and what will happen to it when the star stops shining.

An astrophysicist cannot travel to look at a star close up, so everything they know comes from looking at stars through telescopes and other instruments for seeing far out into space. Astrophysicists observe the light coming from stars but also other things like heat, radio waves and X-rays, and use what they see to understand what is happening inside a star to make it shine. Part of their job is to create new instruments that can see stars in new ways.

One of the things astrophysicists want to see is a new star forming from a cloud of gas in deep space. However, this is very hard to see because the baby star does not shine much. Astrophysicists create complicated models using powerful computers to figure out what might be happening in these invisible stars. This gives them clues to look for in order to spot real stars forming in space.

* *

KEY SKILLS:

Data skills – Astrophysicists have to make sense of measurements coming from many different places and correlate the information.

Collaborating – Studying space requires a lot of people all over the world to work together.

Good communication – Telescopes and other instruments are expensive and so astrophysicists must explain why it is very important to build them.

Technological knowhow – Astrophysicists need to understand how their telescopes and instruments work.

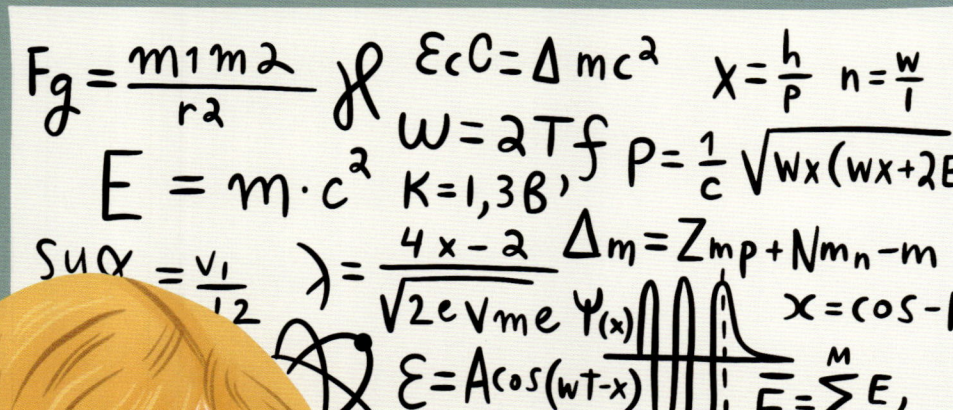

QUANTUM PHYSICIST

What does a Quantum Physicist do?

Quantum physics is the study of the smallest possible objects in the Universe, such as atoms, that combine to make up everything else.

A quantum physicist wants to explain everything in the simplest way possible. That means investigating how energy and matter work inside atoms. Atoms are only a few billionths of a metre long, far too small to see with any microscope. Quantum physicists investigate by studying light and other waves made by atoms and by tracking the behaviour of tiny particles like electrons. They have discovered that things work very strangely at very small sizes. For example, objects can just appear and disappear and be in two places at once!

To make sense of it all, quantum physicists use a complicated maths system called quantum mechanics, which explains what is happening at a scale that is too small to see. Quantum physicists can use this system to build exciting devices, such as light, super-powerful computers and tiny nanomachines.

* *

KEY SKILLS:

Exceptional mathematical skills – Quantum physicists use complicated mathematics to analyse lots of data.

A strong imagination – The quantum world is too tiny to see, so these scientists have to use their imagination to help make sense of what is going on.

Team work – The best results often come when teams of quantum scientists share ideas and work together.

Curiosity – Quantum physics can explain almost everything, so these scientists are interested in almost everything, too.

PARTICLE PHYSICIST

What does a particle physicist do?

A particle physicist studies the many tiny particles that create atoms, radiation and forces that make everything in the Universe work.

A particle physicist works with some of the largest machines in the world. These are called particle accelerators. They are as big as a town! The job of these machines is to make atoms and other particles, like protons or electrons, smash together at very high speeds and break apart. The particle physicists watch to see what happens, and they can then work out what the particles are made from. The answer might be even smaller particles, or strange waves or vibrations of pure energy.

Most scientists work at accelerators or on other experiments for a short while to gather information. They use that information to check their ideas and to come up with new ways to explain how particles form and what they do.

* *

KEY SKILLS:

Eager to learn – Particle physicists are always looking for new ideas from other scientists about how to study particles.

Working with others – Scientists work with a team of engineers and technicians to build and run particle accelerators and other instruments.

Interpreting data – Particle physicists work with complicated measurements made by accelerators and need to make sense of them all.

Good communication – Giant particle accelerators are used by scientists from all over the world and they need to share information with each other.

ASTRONOMER

What does an Astronomer do?

An astronomer is a scientist that investigates space and everything in it from galaxies and nebulae to comets and asteroids.

Astronomy is perhaps the oldest science of them all. People have been studying the way stars move through the night sky for thousands of years. Today's astronomers know a lot more about the Universe, but there is still so much more to discover.

Astronomers observe outer space with huge telescopes. The telescopes are often located high up mountains in desert areas where there are very few clouds to spoil the view. Astronomers visit these places for a short while to make observations and then return home to work out what it means. Astronomers also use space telescopes which can see even further. They are are involved in building space probes that explore the solar system.

KEY SKILLS:

Lots of energy — Astronomers often work all night long at an observatory. They don't get tired easily!

Love of the outdoors — Often telescopes are set up outside - and it can get cold on clear, starry nights!

Attention to detail — Astronomers are looking for tiny details among the stars so they need to look very carefully.

Working with others — These scientists are working with huge telescopes. It takes a team of people to make them work.

METROLOGIST

What does a Metrologist do?

Metrologists are experts in how to measure things. They make sure that the measuring devices other scientists use are accurate.

A metrologist's job is to find the best way to make measurements, and ensure they are accurate. Metrologists are in charge of making sure that every clock ticks out the seconds at the same speed and that rulers and weighing scales always come up with the same results. Scientists know that some things in the Universe always stay the same, and they use these to set up measuring devices.

For example, they tell the time with atomic clocks that measure seconds by the vibrations of atoms. Light always travels at the same speed (it's very fast), and so the distance of one metre is set by how far a beam of light travels in 1/299,792,458th of a second! Metrologists then make very special metal bars that are exactly 1 m long, and these are sent around the world to be copied many time over. Your school rulers are based on these copies!

* *

KEY SKILLS:

Broad knowledge – Metrologists work with many different scientists, helping them to make measurements, so they need to understand all kinds of things.

Attention to detail – To get the most accurate measurements possisble, metrologists need to make sure everything is set up exactly right.

Technical skills – These scientists are responsible for designing very accurate measurement devices.

Interest in numbers — Measurement is all about getting things right, and metrologists use maths and physics to help them achieve that.

METEOROLOGIST

What does a Meteorologist do?

A meteorologist studies the atmosphere to predict the weather and warn people if an extreme storm, flood or drought is on the way.

The job of a meteorologist is to create weather forecasts for a place and time. The forecast could be for a small region or city or for entire country or continent. It could predict what will happen with the weather over the next three hours or over several weeks. To understand how weather like wind, rain, snow, thunder and lightning form – and when it happens – meteorologists need to gather a lot of information about the air. They use weather stations to collect data such as the temperature, pressure and sunshine in an area. The station works automatically and sends data to a central weather centre.

There are weather stations all over the world, up mountains, floating out at sea and on uninhabited islands. Satellites flying high over the world also collect weather data. Meteorologists use all this data to create a computer model that copies the way the real atmosphere creates weather. The model shows meteorologists how the weather is likely to change tomorrow, next week and in the future.

✳ ✳

KEY SKILLS:

Computer skills — Meteorologists use supercomputers to forecast the weather.

Understanding data — Meteorologists work with vast amounts of data that measure the air conditions.

Mathematical knowledge — Meteorologists create complex mathematical systems that help to predict how the atmosphere will change and form clouds or rain.

Team work — Forecasting the weather involves thousands of scientists all over the world!

ACOUSTICIAN

What does an Acoustician do?

Acousticians study sound and other kinds of vibrations. They help create devices and systems that make sounds louder and clearer – and block out unwanted noises.

An acoustician is an expert in acoustics, which is the study of sound. Part of the job of an acoustician is to investigate what sound is and how it behaves. Sound is a vibration or wave travelling in the air. An acoustician also studies the way sound waves move through water, rocks, and other materials. Acousticians often work in anechoic chambers, which are the quietest places on the planet. The walls are lined with soft material that soaks up the sound waves so they do not bounce back as an echo. Inside these chambers, acousticians can study one sound wave at a time, without it getting mixed up with echoes.

Acousticians use what they know about sound to create better microphones and loudspeakers. Noise-cancelling headphones, which block out unwanted sounds, only work thanks to acousticians. An acoustician helps wherever sound is important, such as when designing new buildings, at loud concerts or noisy airports or when investigating the sounds recorded at a crime scene.

* *

KEY SKILLS:

Careful worker – Acoustic equipment is very precise and must be used in exactly the right way.

Team player – Acousticians are often working with other experts who need help to manage sounds.

Good communicator – An acoustician needs to be good at explaining how sounds work so they can fix acoustic problems.

Technical knowhow – These scientists are experts in making and using equipment for recording and playing back sounds.

OPTICAL SCIENTIST

What does an Optical Scientist do?

Optics is the study of light and other kinds of radiation (which we cannot see). An optical scientist investigates everything about beams of light.

Optical scientists are experts on the way beams of light behave. Often they are working with lasers that produce powerful beams of light or other kinds of radiation, such as infrared or ultraviolet light. The scientists make careful observations on how different kinds of laser beam reflect off certain materials or refract (bend) as they shine through others. The scientists use mirrors, lenses and other instruments to investigate beams. They use electronic detectors to measure the colours and brightness of beams. Optical scientists are investigating the way lasers and other devices can be used to make better machines. They are involved in making more powerful cameras, scanners that see inside the body, and making better screens and televisions.

Optical scientists also work with computer experts and telecommunications engineers to help them make faster Internet connections or new ways software sends messages. Biologists may ask for their help in understanding how animals and plants respond to light.

KEY SKILLS:

Good collaborator – An optical scientist will often be working with other experts, such as engineers and technicians.

Design skills – Optical scientists are involved in creating new devices that use lasers or other lights.

Attention to detail – Optics is a very precise science and equipment for measuring light needs to be set up very accurately.

Educating others – It is important for optical scientists to be able to explain their discoveries to other people.

MATERIALS SCIENTIST

What does a Materials Scientist do?

A materials scientist is an expert in how different materials behave. For example, why are some strong and others are soft? The scientists think about these questions and work to create new materials with special properties.

A materials scientist looks very closely at materials, such as metals, plastics, and concrete. They use powerful microscopes and other instruments to look at the way these materials behave close up. They also have powerful testing equipment that will stretch, squeeze, smash and cut the materials and look to see how they break – if they do break! This type of research shows how strong each material is. It also shows the scientists how the structure of the atoms and crystals inside a material controls how they behave. By learning more about that, materials scientists are then able to make new materials that do useful things.

Thanks to materials scientists, passenger jets and racing cars are made from carbon fibre, not metal. Materials scientists have shown that this new material is just as strong as metal but is also much lighter, so the planes and cars use less fuel. Materials scientists also create smart materials. For example, a smart material might change shape when it gets hot – but always switches back when it cools down again.

* *

KEY SKILLS:

A wide range of interests – Materials are used in everything we make, so materials scientists are interested in understanding how lots of different things work.

Puzzle solving – When materials break it is up to a materials scientist to piece together the clues to explain how it happened.

Good collaborator – Materials scientists are often working with engineers and designers to help them figure out how to build things.

A strong imagination – A lot of what is going on inside a material is impossible to see and so these scientists have to imagine it based on what they know.

CLIMATE SCIENTIST

What does a Climate Scientist do?

A climate scientist investigates how different parts of the world have different climates – some are hot and dry, while others are cold or rainy.

Climate scientists look at how a place gets certain kinds of weather over many years. The Sahara is a desert because it has a hot and dry climate — although it can rain, hail and even snow there sometimes. The Amazon is a steamy jungle because it rains there almost every day but is also always very warm. While meteorologists look to see what the weather is doing over a few days, a climate scientist investigates what has been happening to weather over centuries. They want to know how the atmosphere is changing, especially as people are now putting problem gases into the air, such as carbon dioxide and methane.

Climate scientists collect air from a long time ago, often in bubbles trapped in ice that froze many hundreds of years ago. They can compare this with the air today. The scientists also use some of the world's most powerful computers to help them understand how the climate has changed in the past, and how it is changing now, and causing problems like floods, wildfires and giant storms.

* *

KEY SKILLS:

Educating others — Climate change is a very important subject and climate scientists are good at explaining it to the public.

Computer skills — These scientists work with supercomputers to figure out how the climate works.

Working outdoors — Climate scientists sometimes work in wild, outdoor places, often in extreme conditions.

Helping others — The work of climate scientists helps people avoid the dangers of extreme weather.

CONDENSED MATTER PHYSICIST

What does a Condensed Matter Physicist do?

Condensed matter physicists research everything about solids and liquids. What they discover is used to make new materials and clever technology.

Every solid and liquid has a special set of properties. Some can be electrified, others are magnetic and some can switch from being hard or soft. It is the job of a condensed matter physicist to understand why. They look at the way the atoms are arranged inside. Sometimes the atoms are locked into rigid crystals but in other substances they can shift around and flow. The physicists figure out how the atoms are arranged by shining X-rays or beams of particles at them. They also test how the properties change as the substance is heated up, cooled down, stretched, hit with lasers ... the list is very long and a condensed matter physicist is interested in it all!

Condensed matter physics is used to make better magnets, video screens, microchips and batteries. Condensed matter physicists also work in nanotechnology, helping to build tiny machines constructed from just a few hundred atoms.

* *

KEY SKILLS:

Strong imagination – Condensed matter physicists cannot see the atoms in action so they have to use their imaginations to figure what is going on!

Enjoy collaborating – These scientists work together, sharing what they know so everyone can make as many discoveries as possible.

Curiosity – Condensed matter physicists study anything that is liquid or solid and have many things to learn about.

Full of ideas – With such a large number of things to investigate, these scientists are always coming up with new ideas for research.

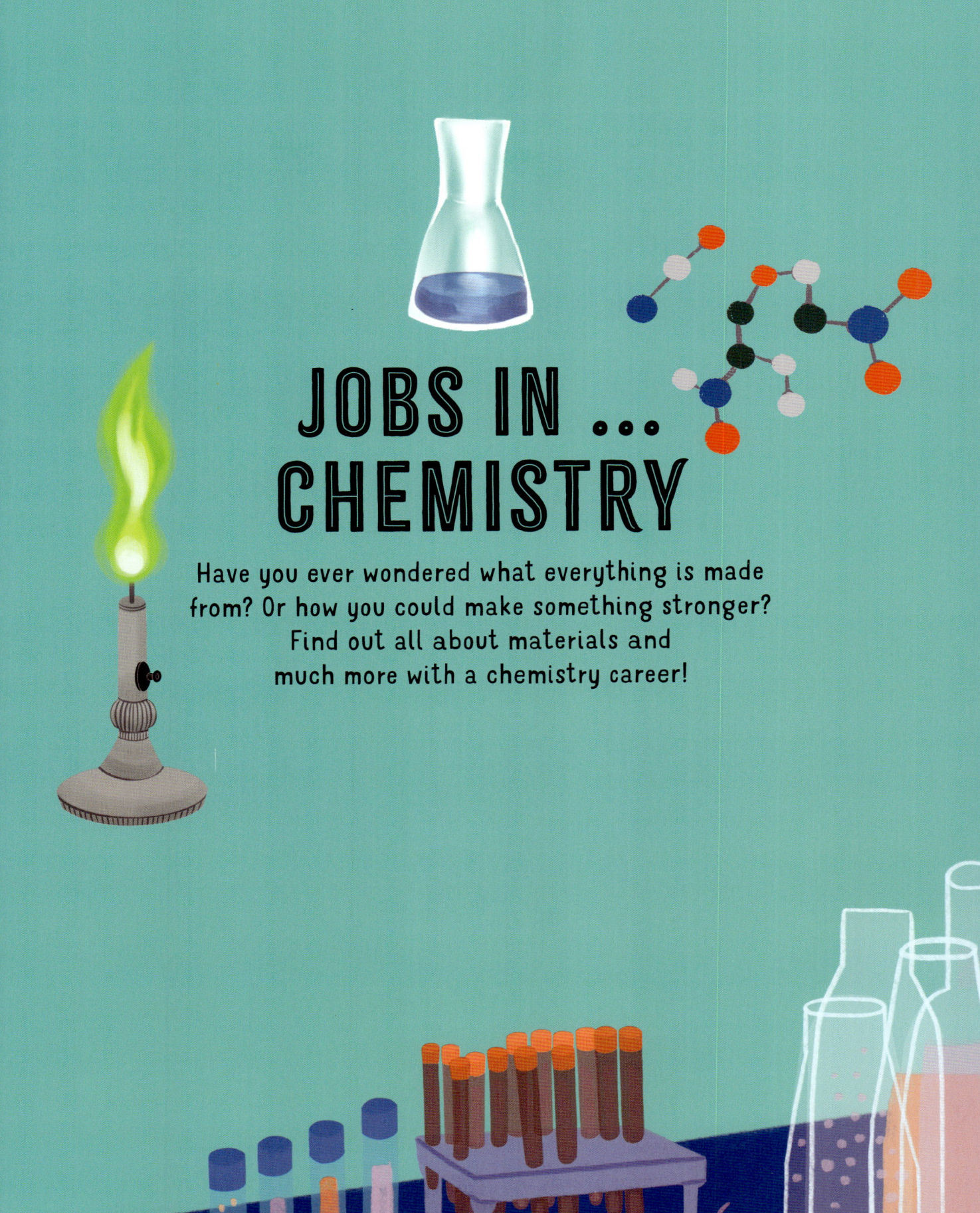

JOBS IN ... CHEMISTRY

Have you ever wondered what everything is made from? Or how you could make something stronger? Find out all about materials and much more with a chemistry career!

BIOCHEMIST

What does a Biochemist do?

A biochemist investigates the chemical changes that are taking place inside a living body.

A biochemist is interested in biology, the science of life, as well as chemistry. A living body, including yours, is kept alive by thousands of chemical reactions. Together these reactions are called metabolism. Biochemists work a lot in a laboratory. They use lasers, microscopes and other complicated instruments to investigate chemicals taken from cells and bodies. It was biochemists who figured out how nerves and the brain send messages, how we digest our food, and why muscles change shape. A biochemist is often involved in creating new medicines. They test how the medicine works inside the body.

A biochemist can show how a problem with metabolism creates an illnesses – and then suggests how to fix the problem. Biochemists also look at how the chemicals that are made in the body could be used in other ways.

* *

KEY SKILLS:

An interest in biology (as well as chemistry) – Biochemistry is the study of the chemistry happening inside living things.

Good at solving puzzles – There are thousands of reactions happening in the body all the time so biochemists must figure out how to study each one.

Handling facts and figures – Biochemistry involves using data to understand how human bodies work.

Good team member – Biochemists spend a lot of time discussing their work with each other and coming up with new ideas.

CHEMICAL ENGINEER

What does a Chemical Engineer do?

A chemical engineer figures out the way simple ingredients can be made into more useful substances in large amounts in a factory.

A chemical engineer uses their knowledge of chemical reactions to create ways of making all kinds of useful things, such as plastics, fabrics and electricity. A chemical engineer is not thinking about how to make these things in a laboratory. Instead they are working on a huge scale in factories, power stations and chemical plants.

A chemical engineer's job is to figure out how to make each product as efficiently as possible. That means using just the right amount of ingredients so as little as possible is wasted. The engineer calculates how hot or fast the reaction needs to be to make it work best. Often a chemical engineer will need to design new equipment for the factory to use, or figure out how to make the old machines work more efficiently.

KEY SKILLS:

Interest in machines – Chemical engineers work in huge industrial plants filled with many different machines all working together.

Likes working with others – Chemical engineering is a big job and so most of the work is done by larger teams of people working together.

Obeying rules – A chemical plant is full of dangerous materials, and so the engineers must always make sure it is running safely by following rules.

Good communicator – The work of chemical engineers is complicated and they have to spend time explaining it to people who are not experts.

ANALYTICAL CHEMIST

What does an Analytical Chemist do?

It is the job of an analytical chemist to investigate a substance and find out exactly what chemicals are in it.

The word analytical comes from a Greek term that means to 'break apart'. An analytical chemist is a bit like a science detective. They must break up a sample of chemicals into its many different parts and figure out what each one is. Sometimes an analytical chemist works for real detectives helping to investigate the chemicals left behind during a crime.

Analytical chemistry is also very important in the food industry for checking exactly what substances are in different foods. An analytical chemist works in a very advanced laboratory where they can carry out many different tests. One common test is to make a substance burn. The colours of light in the flames are a good clue as to what chemicals are inside. Another important laboratory machine is the mass spectrometer. This uses powerful magnets and electrical fields to weigh all the different chemicals in a substance.

* *

KEY SKILLS:

Attention to detail – Analytical chemists are always looking for clues about what might be in a sample of material.

Problem solver – Analytical chemistry is like solving a mystery with a lot of unknown facts to discover and piece together.

Careful worker – An analytical chemist must work carefully to ensure they do not make mistakes and come up with the wrong answers.

Interested in many topics – Analytical chemistry is used for many different reasons and an analytical chemist needs to understand all of them.

TOXICOLOGIST

What does a Toxicologist do?

A toxicologist is an expert on poisons and other dangerous chemicals that can damage the body.

A toxicologist investigates chemicals known as toxins. Toxins can interfere with the way a living body works, so it becomes unwell and even dies. A toxicologist studies chemicals to find out how safe they are. Some chemicals are highly toxic and just tiny amounts of them can be dangerous. However, other substances only become toxic in large amounts and a toxicologist works out exactly how much is needed to be dangerous.

Toxicologists perform their tests in laboratories but they will also spend time collecting samples from many different places. For example, they are looking for toxins in air, soil, water supplies, around building sites and at sewage works. When the police find a dead body, they will always ask a toxicologist to tell them what chemicals are in the blood. This may reveal what the person was doing before they died – and how they might have died.

KEY SKILLS:

Good communicator – A toxicologist often has to explain what they have discovered to people in a clear way.

Likes working with data – Toxicologists must use mathematics to figure out if a certain chemical is harmful to people.

Highly organised – Blood and other samples will not last very long, and so toxicologists must do their work quickly and efficiently.

Being in a team – Toxicologists are often part of a group working on a problem together.

PHARMACOLOGIST

What does a Pharmacologist do?

A pharmacologist is an expert on the chemicals used as medicines.

A pharmacologist's job is to understand how the chemical in a medicine changes the way the body works. One big change is that the medicine stops the body being unwell and cures the illness. However, sometimes the chemical will also do other things, known as a side-effect. A pharmacologist uses their knowledge of biochemistry and medicine to figure out everything that the medicine does. It is their job to run trials for each drug and figure out if the medicine is safe for everyone to use.

Sometimes sick people take several medicines at the same time. A hospital pharmacologist will help them if the different medicines interfere with each other. While some pharmacologists work in hospitals with patients, others work in laboratories designing new medicines. They also research how an old medicine created for one illness might be used for treating a completely different one.

KEY SKILLS:

Computer skills – Pharmacologists work with a lot of data and use computers to make sense of it all.

Communication – It is vital that pharmacologists can explain how medicines work and how they should be used to doctors and patients.

Enjoys working with people – Pharmacologists test new medicines in large trials that use members of the public.

Good at mathematics – Complex calculations are used to check how effective new medicines are and whether they are safe to use.

ORAGNIC CHEMIST

What does an Organic Chemist do?

An organic chemist studies the many different substances that contain carbon.

Carbon is a very special substance. Its atoms can link up in different ways to form rings, long chains and branching structures. As a result, most of the chemicals known to science – about 90 per cent of them – contain carbon. Organic chemists study carbon chemicals and learn how to make new ones with unique shapes. So far they have created about 20 million of them! Organic chemicals made in laboratories or in factories include plastics and artificial fabrics like nylon.

Organic chemicals are also used as medicines, paints and soaps. The word organic means 'from life'. Almost all of the chemicals in a living body contain carbon (so biochemistry is closely linked to organic chemistry). All the other organic chemicals found in nature come from the remains of dead plants, animals and other forms of life. The most important supply is crude oil, which contains many thousands of different organic chemicals.

KEY SKILLS:

Likes teamwork – Organic chemists like to discuss their ideas and work together to try out new things.

Creative thinker — Carbon chemistry is very varied, and organic chemists come up with all kinds of new molecules.

Methodical work – It takes many steps to create new carbon chemicals and each one must be carried out in the right way, in an exact order.

Great laboratory skills – Organic chemists use a wide range of equipment, including heaters, chillers and mixers to build their chemicals.

FORENSIC SCIENTIST

What does a Forensic Scientist do?

A forensic scientist uses chemistry and other sciences to work out what happened during a crime.

When the police uncover a crime scene, the first people they call are the forensic scientists. They make sure nothing is touched at the scene until they arrive. Forensics is a way of using all kinds of science to prove who committed a crime, and many specialists are involved. A very big part of forensic science is analysing the chemicals left at the scene. This might be the rubber left by a car tyre speeding away, flecks of paint, or strands of fabric. Crime scene investigators collect these materials, being careful to make sure no other chemicals get added by mistake.

Back at the crime lab, the forensic scientists analyse the samples. The chemicals in each sample - the rubber, paint and thread - show where they were made. The forensic scientists can then tell detectives what to look for when searching for suspects.

KEY SKILLS:

Attention to detail – It is very important that crime scene investigators spot every clue to help catch the criminals.

Caring for others – The work of forensic scientists can have a big effect on other people and so the scientists must be as accurate as they can.

Communication skills – A forensic scientist must explain what they have discovered at a crime scene in a clear and precise way.

Being patient – It takes many scientists working together to solve a crime mystery and that means forensic scientists are often waiting for others to do their job before they can start theirs.

PHYSICAL CHEMIST

What does a Physical Chemist do?

A physical chemist studies how atoms bond together and break apart during chemical reactions.

A physical chemist is interested in what is happening during a chemical reaction. Every common substance from water and sand to salt and plastic is created by a chemical reaction. All those substances are made up of certain atoms connected in a particular shape, called a molecule. During a chemical reaction, the atoms in molecules break apart and rearrange into different shapes, making new molecules and new substances. A physical chemist watches this process happen. However, the molecules are too small to see, so scientists use lasers and other high-tech equipment to pick up signs of what the atoms are doing.

Physical chemists look at how strongly atoms bond together and how different molecules behave. The discoveries made by physical chemists are used by all other chemists to work out how to build new molecules and create tests for other substances.

KEY SKILLS:

Understanding mathematics – Physical chemistry looks at energy and forces and that means doing a lot of calculations.

Wide knowledge of sciences – Physical chemistry is linked to physics, materials science and engineering.

Interested in technology – This science uses the very latest sensors and equipment to make more accurate measurements.

Like working with others – Physical scientists are often part of a team, working out small parts of a bigger puzzle.

NANOTECHNOLOGIST

What does a Nanotechnologist do?

A nanotechnologist designs and builds the world's tiniest machines made from just a few atoms.

A nanotechnologist creates devices that are measured in nanometres. One nanometre is one billionth of a metre, or a millionth of a millimetre! At this size objects contain only a few hundred atoms. A nanotechnologist works in a very clean laboratory to make sure their builds are not damaged by dirt. The atoms are far too small to see, and too small to pick up. Instead a nanotechnologist can use an incredibly fine metal spike to give each atom a tiny push or pull. Very carefully they assemble different machines. The machines include electrical switches or medical sensors, tiny containers for holding other chemicals, or ultra-fine smart fabrics.

Nanotechnologists use computers to design their tiny machines and figure out the best way to make them. They often need to create new kinds of equipment for constructing their designs and testing how they work.

KEY SKILLS:

Careful worker – Nanotechnology is so small that even the tiniest mistake means the process has to start all over again.

Enjoys being in a team – A nanotechnologist will be part of a team that works together. It takes a lot of people to make something so small!

Well organised – Because they work with things that they cannot see, nanotechnologists make careful plans so they can get the job done.

Good communicator – Nanotechnology is a new area of science that can be used in many ways, so the experts need to explain all the new things it can do.

COMPUTATIONAL CHEMIST

What does a Computational Chemist do?
A computational chemist uses computers to investigate molecules and chemical reactions.

A computational chemist does not work in a laboratory with test tubes and gas burners. They do not mix up chemicals and see how they react. Instead they create a model of a chemical reaction and run it in a computer. To do this they tell the computer what other chemists have discovered about how real-life atoms and molecules behave. Using a computer is much faster than doing lab experiments. Computational chemists can carry out hundreds of them everyday.

Using a computer allows the scientists to see the tests that are worth looking at more closely. In the real world reactions occur in a tiny fraction of a second. A computer version of a reaction can be slowed right down to watch what is happening in more detail. Computational chemists can also investigate reactions that are very expensive or very dangerous to do in real life. And they can also be the first to try out new reactions that no one else has ever done.

* *

KEY SKILLS:

Expert programming skills – The models used by computational chemists have to be very accurate or they will not work properly.

Creativity — A computational chemist can build any chemical they can imagine in a computer and see what it does.

Solving problems – A computer model is a good place to start investigating a science mystery.

A wide interest in sciences – A computational chemist can create a model to understand any chemical in any system, from gas in the air to the lava inside a volcano.

NUCLEAR CHEMIST

What does a Nuclear Chemist do?

A nuclear chemist investigates an atom's core, or nucleus.

Atoms are made up of a tiny core, or nucleus, surrounded by a cloud of particles called electrons. In most chemical reactions, the electrons around the atom are doing all the work, making the atoms stick together or fly apart. The nucleus always stays the same. However, in a nuclear reaction, the nucleus does change and it gives out a blast of energy and fast-moving particles.

Another name for these reactions is radioactivity, and the atoms that react like this can be very dangerous. A nuclear chemist knows how to stay safe while studying radioactivity. They keep the radioactive chemicals inside thick containers, they wear protective suits and they have detectors that measure how much radioactivity there is. A nuclear chemist's job is to keep us all safe from both natural and human-made radioactivity. They also study how radioactivity can be used in medicine and to make electricity.

KEY SKILLS:

Likes being part of a team – Nuclear reactions usually take place inside large, complicated laboratories and power stations, where many scientists and engineers work together.

Well organised – Radioactive chemicals are dangerous and so nuclear chemists always prepare well before using them.

Sticks to the rules – There are many strict controls on radioactive materials and nuclear chemists understand why they are important.

Good at mathematics – Nuclear chemists are using physics as well as chemistry to understand reactions and that requires complicated calculations.

LAB TECHNICIAN

What does a Lab Technician do?

A lab technician looks after the equipment and materials used by chemists in experiments.

A lab technician is an important part of the science team at a chemistry laboratory. They work with the other scientists to plan how experiments will be carried out. It is the technician's job to make sure that the laboratory is a safe place to work. The technician organises all the equipment and the chemicals needed for the experiments. They are also in charge of making sure the different chemicals are handled carefully and disposed of safely.

A very important role of the technician is to calibrate the lab's measuring devices, such as the weighing scales or thermometers. This means that they regularly check that whatever reading a device gives is always true. The technician will also measure out the chemicals for each experiment and check that they are pure. The technician will keep the laboratory stocked with everything it needs. If another scientist needs something unusual, then the lab technician will find it for them.

KEY SKILLS:

Enjoys working with others – A lab technician is always a member of a larger team working on many different science projects.

Attention to detail – Other scientists rely on the technician to make accurate measurements and set up equipment properly.

Well organised – There are many different experiments happening in a lab, so the technician is busy all the time and need to plan well.

Problem solver – A scientific laboratory is full of equipment, people and materials, and it's up to the lab technician to keep everything, and everybody, working.

JOBS IN... TECHNOLOGY AND ENGINEERING

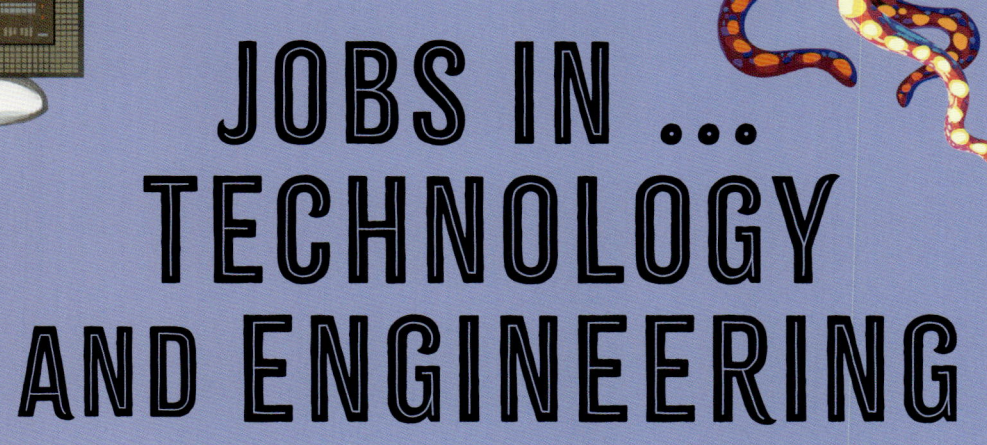

Engineers take the discoveries made by scientists and put them to work. They create new technologies that make our lives better. Find out the variety of different roles in this field and which kind of engineer may suit you.

MECHANICAL ENGINEER

What does a Mechanical Engineer do?

A mechanical engineer designs and builds engines and other machines that have a lot of moving parts.

A mechanical engineer designs and builds any device that has moving parts, such as cars, robots and factory machines. They are experts in how engines work and in the different materials that can be used to build machines. They design each machine using a CAD (computer-aided design) system.

The engineer uses CAD to draw an exact version of the machine. Then the computer can make the design move and test how it works. Next, the engineer builds a real-life version, called a prototype. The prototype is tested in many ways to find out what needs to be improved. Engineers are very careful about the design and testing. It takes a long time before a final design is ready, but the engineer is sure it will do its job very well.

* *

KEY SKILLS:

Broad knowledge – These engineers have to work with all kinds of technology.

Attention to detail – Mechanical engineers have to make sure that they build their machines exactly as they are designed.

Works well in a team – When they have a large project to complete, engineers often work together in a team to get the job done.

Having patience – Designing and building complicated machines takes time.

ELECTRICAL ENGINEER

What does an Electrical Engineer do?

An electrical engineer is an expert in how to make electricity and use it to power machines.

Electricity is incredibly useful. Most machines are powered by it, from a wristwatch to a car, and they all work thanks to electrical engineers. An electrical engineer designs the circuits that send electricity around the machine. They make sure the device gets enough power, but not too much that it becomes unsafe. An electrical engineer may design completely new components, such as batteries or safety switches, to make machines work better. An electrical engineer can also work at power plants where electricity is being produced.

Today, new places for generating electricity, such as solar farms and wind turbines, are being constructed all over the world. An important job is to figure out the best way to transmit this electricity to where it is needed. An electrical engineer works on the electricity grid. This is the name for the long cables, pylons, and other systems that link us all to a power supply.

KEY SKILLS:

Mathematical skills – Complicated calculations are needed to understand how electricity behaves.

Enjoys being in a team – Electrical engineers often work in teams that each focus on a particular problem to solve.

Creativity – Engineers need to think outside of the box to solve problems.

Research skills – This area of engineering is always testing out new ideas.

AEROSPACE ENGINEER

What does an Aerospace Engineer do?

An aerospace engineer works to make things that fly through the air and travel into space.

Flying machines, such as aircraft and space rockets, are difficult to build. They need to travel very fast but they cannot be very heavy. They need to slice through the air easily but also be very strong so they do not break apart. An aerospace engineer's job is to figure out how to make these complicated machines. As well as using computer designs, an aerospace engineer tests the design of a plane in a wind tunnel. These have a very powerful fan for blowing air around a small model of an aircraft. This shows what would happen if a real aircraft was flying very fast.

Aerospace engineers are also involved in designing and testing powerful jet and rocket engines as well as scramjets, which are a mixture of both types working together. Aerospace engineers are involved in creating the computer control systems for aircraft, which makes them easier and safer to fly - and allows them to fly by themselves, even at take-off and landing.

KEY SKILLS:

Hard working - A lot of people want to work as aerospace engineers, building rockets and planes, and the ones that succeed work very hard to get there.

Excited by big projects - Aerospace engineers take on some of the most difficult tasks, such building spacecraft or designing passenger jets.

Good team player - Aircraft and rockets are complicated machines and so many engineers are needed to work on them.

Communication skills - Aerospace engineers need to explain how their designs will work to many different people.

CONSTRUCTION ENGINEER

What does a Construction Engineer do?

A construction engineer figures out how to make skyscrapers, bridges and other large building projects.

Constructing a building takes a large group of people. The construction engineer works with the architect, who has created the main building design. The engineer works out the best way to make the architect's ideas a reality. They must check what materials are needed. Will they be strong enough or too heavy? The construction engineer then plans how the structure will be put together by the builders.

A construcution engineer makes sure the construction process is safe and efficient so that every part is made in the correct order. This way of working is used for houses and apartment blocks as well as for much bigger projects, such as a tunnel, bridge or dam. As the building is being constructed, the engineer checks everything is being done correctly. If they find problems, then the project stops until it is fixed.

KEY SKILLS:

Great at communication – Construction engineers need to make sure everyone understands the building plan.

Well organised – Big construction projects have many stages and the engineer needs to be ready for each one.

Enjoys teamwork – As with most types of engineers, construction engineers often work in a team.

Follows rules – A construction engineer must make sure that everything being built follows all the safety rules.

MICROCHIP ENGINEER

What does a Microchip Engineer do?
This kind of engineer designs the microchips used in computers, and also creates the complicated machines that make them.

Microchips are about the size of a chewy sweet, but they have millions – even billions – of tiny parts to them. The chip is a piece of pure silicon and the many parts are laid down on top. A microchip engineer designs where all the parts go, and how they connect. Each component can only be seen with a very powerful microscope, so the engineers start with a huge computer design, which is like a magnified map of the surface of the chip. The chip's job is to be a computer processor. Electrical signals run between the components according to a set of rules created by the computer program.

Microchip engineers will use computers to test out designs to see if they do their job properly before making chips for real. A microchip factory is called a fabricator. It uses complicated machines to build all those tiny components. Microchip engineers are involved in building new fabricators that can create better and more advanced chips.

KEY SKILLS:
Careful worker – Designing a microchip takes a lot of slow and careful work. Any mistakes have to be spotted and fixed.

Computer skills – A microchip engineer has a good knowledge of how computers work in general.

Very patient – Engineers can work on one microchip design for years. There is a lot to get right!

Innovator – Microchip engineers are always looking for new components and designs that will make chips work better.

CRYPTOGRAPHER

What does a Cryptographer do?

A cryptographer is an expert in codes that are used to keep important information secret.

When we send messages or buy things on the web, we rely on codes to keep our data secret. Without these codes, criminals could steal our information and even pretend to be us. A cryptographer creates the codes and makes sure they cannot be broken. A code is a way of turning ordinary words or numbers into a new form that hides the true meaning. To decode these messages, a person needs the key. As long as the key is kept secret then the coded messages are safe. However, when we send messages through the Internet, everyone can see them.

The main job of a cryptographer is to create code so that the keys to that code can be sent through the Internet in a way that cannot be stolen by criminals. The codes that do this use some complicated mathematics. It would take a powerful computer many years to break, or crack, the code. However, another part of a cryptographer's job is to figure out new ways to crack these codes. They want to find any problems or weaknesses before the criminals do, and fix them quickly.

KEY SKILLS:

Good at mathematics – The strongest codes use mathematics and cryptographers need to know how they work, and how they might be cracked.

Being creative – It takes a lot of imagination to figure out a brand new code system.

Problem-solver – Cracking codes is the ultimate puzzle, and cryptographers like solving puzzles.

Being curious – Cryptographers look for new ideas everywhere.

GENETIC ENGINEER

What does a Genetic Engineer do?
A genetic engineer changes the genes in living things to make them more useful.

Genetics is the study of how living things handle the instructions for making a body. These instructions are called genes, and everyone gets their genes from their parents. How genes work, especially the genes of humans and other complex animals, is still being discovered. However, scientists know a lot more about simpler life, such as bacteria. A genetic engineer takes the genes from one type of living thing and puts it into another type. For example, the gene used by jellyfish for making them glow in the dark has been added to mice. Now those mice glow in the dark as well!

Genetic engineers mostly work with plants to make crops that grow better in dry or cold conditions. They also engineer bacteria so they have the gene to produce valuable medicines and other substances. The new gene is added by a special set of chemicals called enzymes. Genetic engineers are always researching new ways to reorganise genes.

KEY SKILLS:

Careful and patient – It can take several attempts for genetic engineering to work, so these experts need to take their time.

Enjoys communicating difficult ideas – Genetic engineering is not an easy topic to understand, and the engineers need to explain it all carefully.

Follows the rules – Genetic engineering is carefully controlled and follows strict sets of rules.

Full of ideas – Genetic engineers can use their methods to tackle a huge number of problems.

EPIDEMIOLOGIST

What does an Epidemiologist do?

An epidemiologist is an expert in how diseases spread and how they can be prevented.

Some diseases are infectious, which means a sick person passes them on to other people, who also get ill. Common infectious diseases include flu, covid and measles. Although these diseases may not be serious for many people, they can make some people very ill. Therefore, doctors need to know how many people have a disease and how it spreads through a city, or country – or the world. This is the job of an epidemiologist. Epidemiologists study each disease to learn how it spreads and they can calculate how quickly it is passed on. When a disease is more common than usual it causes an epidemic. (A pandemic is when there are many epidemics across the whole world.)

Epidemiologists work to slow down the spread of the diseases. They explain to people how to stay safe and they organise vaccinations which stop or slow the spread. For the most dangerous diseases, epidemiologists search for potential sufferers and take them to hospital before they can spread it to others.

KEY SKILLS:

Mathematical knowledge – Epidemiologists use mathematical models to predict how a disease will spread.

Enjoys working with people – Epidemiologists spend a lot of time with the public during disease outbreaks.

Caring and compassionate – Fighting diseases this way will mean fewer people will get ill and die.

Great communicator – Epidemiologists spend a lot of time explaining how to prevent diseases and stay healthy.

NETWORK ENGINEER

What does a Network Engineer do?

A network engineer organises the connections between computers including the Internet.

Thanks to network engineers, the world is a very connected place. Phones, computers, cars, cameras and even doorbells are now linked together through the Internet. The internet is a vast computer network, where our devices are connected by wires, by WiFi and via satellite links, and all of them have been designed and built by network engineers. A computer network is not just about connections. Networks also include hubs called routers that organise where all the messages and information goes. Engineers also build security systems that protect the information.

A network engineer designs and builds new networks. They could be for a single building, a large organisation or a whole city. There are also networks running under the seabed. As well as making new networks, the engineer spends a lot of time testing and fixing the ones we have already.

KEY SKILLS:

Good planner – Network engineers must make sure everyone knows what they are doing before changing the network.

Enjoy collaborating – Network engineers often work with other experts as they construct the network.

Likes a big project – New networks are being built all the time and they need engineers to maintain them for years.

Attention to detail – A network engineer needs to spot mistakes and fix them so the network keeps on working.

WEB DEVELOPER

What does a Web Developer do?

A web developer creates websites and other services and features used on the Web and in apps.

The Web is short for World Wide Web, which is a vast collection of information. It's everything from videos and games to dictionaries and weather forecasts and a lot more. This information is held on computers all over the world. As long as they have an Internet connection, anyone can look at this information as a website. A web developer is the expert that creates a website. They design how the words and pictures will look, but a web page does a lot more than that. The developer can add features like video, sound, animations and games. The developer will test the website to check that it works well on all kinds of devices.

Web developers are also involved in adding systems to websites that record who visits the pages and what they interact with. Many of the apps that are used on phones and tablets are based on website technology and web developers work on these too.

KEY SKILLS:

Being creative – As well as being a technical job, a web developer is also a creative person.

Listening skills – Web developers do best if they listen carefully to what their customers want the website to do.

Great computer skills – Web developers need to understand how different kinds of computers work.

Problem-solver – Often a website can develop a problem. The web developer has to find the cause of the problem and fix it fast.

SPORTS TECHNOLOGIST

What does a Sports Technologist do?

A sports technologist designs improved sports equipment to make players better and safer.

From the balls, bats and rackets to the footwear and clothing used by athletes, technology is very important to sports. For world champions, the correct equipment can easily make the difference between winning and losing. For people that do sports for fun, good equipment makes it safer and more enjoyable. A sports technologist is an expert in how the human body moves. They will use sensors and cameras to collect information about how athletes behave while they are competing. This information helps to show if an athlete is at risk of certain injuries. The technologists can then suggest new clothing or equipment, which may help to prevent injury.

A sports technologist also researches ways of improving equipment like golf clubs, football boots, and tennis rackets. They test new designs that work better with the way the sportsperson moves, or uses new materials that are stronger or lighter.

KEY SKILLS:

Likes working with people – This area of engineering is all about building technology for people to use.

Good communication – A sports technologist must spend a lot of time talking to sportspeople and athletes.

Attention to detail – Even a tiny improvement from new technology can make a big difference.

Loves innovation – A sports technologist works everyday to make sport both more fun and safer.

SOFTWARE DEVELOPER

What does a Software Developer do?

A software developer designs computer programs and writes the code for them.

Computers need programs to work. Another name for a program is software, and it is produced by software developers. They are also sometimes called software engineers. Developing software involves several steps. First, the developer makes a plan for what the new software will do. They then check with the people who will use this software to see if the plan fits with what they want to do. Next, a detailed design for the software will be created that sets out how the program will work. After that, the software is written in a programming language, or code, that the computer will understand.

A software developer is an expert in using these languages. Now the software needs to be tested to see if it works like the design said it should. The developer will mend any problems. Finally the software will be ready for people to use. The developer is still involved in fixing any issues by writing updates to the software. Eventually, the developer will make a new version of the program. They create a new plan that improves the original – and the process starts again!

KEY SKILLS:

Team player – Software developers have to work with a large team when building complicated software.

Attention to detail – The best software consists of many details that all work well.

Willing to rethink – Software testing often shows that changes and new ideas are needed to make it work.

Being focussed – Writing computer code takes a lot of concentration.

ROBOTICIST

What does a Roboticist do?
A roboticist designs and builds robots and programs how they work.

Robotics is the type of engineering that creates robots and other machines that have complex moving parts and use computers to control their movements. Robots can look like animals or people, but the rovers sent to explore Mars are also robotic machines, as are driverless cars. Roboticists make them all. A roboticist is involved in all parts of the process in making a robot. They design it using a computer, organising how it will move and how it will be powered.

Robots are built to run by themselves, so the roboticist also designs a control system. That means adding sensors and cameras so the robot can detect what is going on around it. After all that, the roboticist makes a prototype and tests it to see if the robot works properly. Roboticists often copy living bodies to make their robot designs. There are robots that move like fish, kangaroos and dogs. Some human-like robots even have faces that talk and pull expressions just like ours!

* *

KEY SKILLS:

Has a wide range of skills – Roboticists are experts in mechanical engineering, software development and electrical engineering, plus much more!

A good imagination – Robot designers can be inspired by anything they see around them.

Perserwernace – It takes many attempts and design changes before a robot is finished.

Hard worker – A lot of people would like to be a robot engineer so they have to work hard at being the best.

Index

algae 21
atoms 39, 44, 52, 56, 75, 76, 79, 80

bacteria 21, 25, 98

climate 13, 22, 55
code 97, 109

dark energy 35
DNA 14, 25, 26

ecosystem 13, 17, 18, 29
echo 48
electricity 63, 80, 89
enzymes 98

fabricator 94

insects 18

lasers 51, 56, 60, 75

magnets 56, 64
medicine 21, 60, 68, 71, 80
methane 55
microscopes 18, 21, 25, 39, 52, 60
migration 30

nanotechnology 56, 76

particle accelerator 40
poison 67
prototype 86

radioactivity 80
remote controlled cameras 9
robots 110

scramjet 90
solar farm 89
submersible 22

supercomputers 35, 47

telescope 36, 43

ultraviolet light 51

vaccine 25, 101

weather 13, 42, 47, 55

X-rays 36, 55

First published in Great Britain in 2025 by Wayland
Copyright © Hodder and Stoughton Limited, 2025

All rights reserved.

Editor: Melanie Palmer
Designer: Lisa Peacock

ISBN 978 1 5263 2739 0 (hardback)
ISBN 978 1 5263 2740 6 (paperback)

Illustrator credits:
Alejandra Ruiz: pp9, 45, 100
Alessandra Santielli: pp 12, 53, 82, 92
Anastasiia Panchenko: p103
Brooke O'Neill: pp23, 38, 65, 111
Claudia Marianno: pp15, 37, 81, 88
Jieyu Deng: pp24, 41, 70, 107
Le Naht Vu: pp 26, 54, 70, 91
Ma Pe: pp10, 66, 104
Markia Jenai: pp28, 49, 77, 95
Nathalia Takeyama: pp31, 46, 78, 108
Sue Downing: pp16, 50, 74, 96
Taylor Mobley: pp20, 42, 62, 87
Valerya Miovanova: pp7, 57, 69
Weronika Salach: pp 19, 34, 61, 99

Printed and bound in Dubai

Wayland, an imprint of
Hachette Children's Group
Part of Hodder and Stoughton
Carmelite House
50 Victoria Embankment
London EC4Y 0DZ

An Hachette UK Company
www.hachette.co.uk
www.hachettechildrens.co.uk

The authorised representative in the EEA is Hachette Ireland,
8 Castlecourt Centre, Dublin 15, D15 XTP3, Ireland
(email: info@hbgi.ie)

MIX
Paper | Supporting responsible forestry
FSC® C104740